Love Letters to the Most High God

Life, Struggles, and Spiritual Perspectives Through Poetry

Yvette Mulkey

TaylorMade Publishing
904-323-1334
www.TaylorMadePublishingFL.com
Jacksonville, FL

Copyright © November 2020
Yvette Mulvey
ISBN: 978-1-953526-02-1

Love Letters to the Most High God:
Life, Struggles, and Spiritual Perspectives Through Poetry

All rights reserved.

This book or parts of thereof may not be reproduced in any form, stored in a retrieval system, or transmitted in any form by an y means; electronic, mechanical, photocopy, recording, or otherwise without prior written permission of the publisher or author, except as provided by United States of America copyright.

Published by TaylorMade Publishing, LLC of Florida
November 2020
www.TaylorMadePublishingFL.com

Table of Contents

Dedication	1
Fullness of Joy	2
Warrior King	4
The Wooing	6
Places of Praise	7
Alone	9
Water Walking	10
What I Need	11
Dragon Slayer	12
What Do They Know?	14
Helpmate	15
Vacuity	16
Joie de vivre - El Simchat Gili	17
Intimacy	19
Who You Are	20
Loose	21
Storms	22
Sing	23
Like Gideon	24
This Love	26
You Know Me	27
Rocks	28
I Know Mary	29
The Greatest	30
Preacher	31
Infallible Proof	32
Dancing Before the Lord	33
Tinsel	34
Revival	36
Thankful	37
Adore	39
Endunamoo	40
Youth	42
Dare I	43
Knowing	44
Blurred Vision	45
Messenger	46
Lost	47

I Want	49
Requiem	50
Flying	51
Praise	52
Conquer	53
Reborn	55
Glory	56
I'm Yours	57
Songs of Deliverance	59
Metamorphosis	60
Keeper	62
Demigod	66
Vision	68
Fortunes	69
Ambrosia	71
Not complicated	73
Cape Diem	74
Your Love Is Like	76
Wrestle	77
Creation	79
Beloved	81
Your Love II	83
God	84
Beyond	86
Caterpillars and Butterflies	87
Pneuma	89
Skin	90
Us	91
Hell	93
The Knowing	95
Modern Day Pharisee	96
Your Love III	97
Christian	98
Spirituality	99
Daystar	100
Figs	102
Needy	104
Hand Holding	105
All That's Divine	106
Beautiful Ugly	107

Kite	109
Emancipation	110
Word	112
Broken	113
Mother's Cry - The Hoodie Song	115
So Loved	116
Heaven	117
Raw	118
Speak to Me	119
Shine forth	120
Our Story	122
Gravity	123
What if	124
Still	125
Reality	126
Awaken	128
Gestation	130
About the Author	131

Dedication

This book is dedicated to Romaine Agnes Mulkey and Daniel Felton Mulkey I love you both beyond forever. Like the poet E.E. Cummings the poet wrote, "I carry your heart with me."

To Rose, Erika, Deborah and Tina and all my sister-girls you know who you are thank you for your unrelenting support and nudging.

Fullness of Joy

When my vessel's depleted
And I'm feeling defeated
In you I find fullness of joy

When there's nothing to give
And it's so hard to live
In you I find fullness of joy

When I'm being attacked
With no strength to fight back
In you I find fullness of joy

When I've done all I know
And life's taken its toll
In you I find fullness of joy

When they let go my hand
Cause they don't understand
In you I find fullness of joy

When I can't find my smile
Because I'm hurt for a while
In you I find fullness of joy
When accused and blamed
Scandalized and shamed
In you I find fullness of joy

When I'm stripped to the bone
Then cast out all alone
In you I find fullness of joy

When doubled crossed
And suffering much loss
In you I find fullness of joy
When rocks are thrown
And I'm bruised by my own
In you I find fullness of joy

When they act so superior
Thinking I am inferior
In you I find fullness of joy

When everything crumbles
And my footsteps do stumble
In you I find fullness of joy

Though killed all day
I still boldly say
In you I find fullness of joy

As your sons and your daughters
We are sheep for the slaughter
But in you we find fullness of joy

Cause your love never wanes
Through it all it remains
So in you I find fullness of joy

Through peril and sword
I proclaim you as Lord
And in you I find fullness of joy

Warrior King

It was hard today
And I just wanted to scream
Shut the door on my realities
Escape into a dream

I crawled into my bed sighing
Exhausted and so beat
Feeling weary and worn out
Needing refuge, a retreat

Then I heard a small voice saying
Shall tribulation or distress
Persecution or famine
Or even nakedness

No Christ's love would be there for me
And his mercy and his grace
Have to touch his garment right now
Just the hem down at the base

So I closed my eyes trusting
Asked the Lord to breathe on me
Give back life to my dry bones
Restore my vitality

When my eyes opened to morning
There was one thing that was clear
God would keep me when there's harm
So I did not need to fear

He loves me beyond measure
And he'll advocate my plight
He'll catch hold of my archrivals
And subdue them with his might

He'll reach down into mire
Saving me from the abyss
From the pits where snakes are masters
Where they slither and they hiss

What a love my God does render
So I trust him with my fate
Even when the lion's roaring
And I'm right at hell's own gate

Though life's battles prove so daunting
I can rest in my God's arms
Knowing he's the king of warfare
So I need not be alarmed

The Wooing

You caused the wind to blow against my skin just the way I like it
You had the lightening bugs dance for me
You painted the sky stunning dawns of the morning
You let me see a rainbow over the ocean
You made me cry at your sweetness
You caused me to smile for no reason
You had the songbirds sing outside my window
You had the stars twinkle on clear nights
You indwelled me with the Holy Ghost
You shared with me your goodness
You lifted up my head
You brought me laughter
You gave me words of wisdom
You encouraged me
You healed me on the Sabbath day
You made me feel special
You honored me
You gave me favor
You forgave me
You fought for me
You won me with your wooing

Places of Praise

Deep in the ocean
Where the stingrays' dwell
Where the starfish lays
And there're oyster shells
Where the seahorse gallops
And there're dolphin sounds
Where the great white feeds
And the squid is found
There's praise for you Lord

Deep in the forest
Where the owl is heard
Where the squirrel gathers nuts
And there're lots of birds
Where the deer does run
And possums pounce
Where bears do growl
While rabbits bounce
There's praise for you Lord

Deep in the jungle
Where hyenas laugh
Where rhinos charge
Hippos take their baths
Where wildcats rule
And termites feast
Where the only survivors
Are the stronger beasts
There's praise for you Lord

Among races
Cultures and classes
Within communities
Families and masses
Where there's peace
And where there's war
Among the rich
And among the poor
There's praise for you Lord

Up in the heavens
Beyond where we are
Past the planets
And the farthest star
Where cherubs have wheels
And also wings
There are legions of angels
And celestial beings
There's praise for you Lord

But most of all
Find praise in me
Just like David
I want to be
A "living place" of adulation
Giving you
Sheer exaltation
A worshipper of God divine
A place where you will always find
There's praise for you Lor

Alone

I'll stand alone
And lift your name on high
I'll stand alone
Cause you I won't deny

I'll stand alone
When others worship Baal
I'll stand alone
Through brimstone and through hell

I'll stand alone
Like Noah at the ark
I'll stand alone
In the blackness of the dark

I'll stand alone
When blood does bleed the sun
I'll stand alone
Won't give up and won't run

I'll stand alone
With everything to lose
I'll stand alone
No other choice to choose

I'll stand alone
Until my dying day
I'll stand alone
There's nothing else to say

Water Walking

Show me how to walk on water
It's what I can't perceive
Show me how to walk on water
Transcend what I believe

Show me how to walk on water
Though the winds of storms do blow
Show me how to walk on water
You're the only one who knows

Show me how to walk on water
Take my doubts and reassure
Show me how to walk on water
With each step I am secure

Show me how to walk on water
Let me move upon the sea
Show me how to walk on water
Take the limits off of me

Show me how to walk on water
Let me come to you right now
Show me how to walk on water
Or on shore I'll surely drown

Show me how to walk on water
Without you it's all quicksand
Show me how to walk on water
So forever I will stand

What I Need

Sometimes it's found in the silence
Sometimes it's found in the rest
Often it's found in the stillness
And even in the surrender
Sometimes it's found in the change
And in the acceptance of that change
I've found it at the end of a journey
And among the spoils of war
Sometimes it's found in a message
Or under my Juniper tree
Sometimes it's found with laughter
Or tears wiped away
I've found it in quick escapes
I've found it in lessons learned
Sometimes it's been there all along
And sometimes I really have to search for it
But always, yes always, I find it in you

Dragon Slayer

When I think about the darkness
The place where I did dance
Bewitched by the shadows
Overtaken and entranced

When I think of all the pleasure
I imagine I would gain
And the irony that chocked me
Pleasure temporal, lots of pain

When I think of all the demons
That had me as their muse
How I gave into their bidding
For their service and their use

When I think about the ugly
And the ugliness in me
How I covered it with pretense
And false sincerity

When I think about the breakdown
All the tears that I did cry
Finally calling to you Jesus
Cause I didn't want to die

When I think about the battle
For my life you took your sword
Struck the dragon with your fierceness
Let him know that you are Lord

When I think of my deliverance
How you took me to the dawn
How you let me see a new day
And you told me to live on

When I think of you my hero
How you snatched me from the night
Said never stop my dancing
But do it in the light

When I think of all these things
Like the sun my soul does shine
I am yours my dragon slayer
And forever you are mine

What Do They Know?

What do they know of your love for me?
The passion that you have expressed is like a touch from a gentle breeze
And yet at the same time raw and raging and unabashed
The first time you embraced me I thought that I would die from it
It was too pure, too honest and it threatened to slay me
How could you be so intense?
I want to love you as you love me
If I could break free from this flesh and become one in spirit with you
I would
My beloved, my beloved, what do they know of your love for me?
They weren't there when I was lying in my blood
And you came along with balm for healing
You wiped tears away, and handled my heart with care
You gave me beauty for ashes
You kept all of your promises and gave me a place of rest
They can say what they want, but I know my redeemer lives
What do they know of your love for me?
And your love hasn't changed through the years
Why do you love me so?
You love me now as you loved me then
You've searched out no others, and I can still feel your gaze upon me
Let them laugh
The love I can give I will give to you because you're worthy
I don't care what they say
I am my beloved and my beloved is mine
What do they know of your love for me?

Helpmate

I remember how you came
With an extended hand
I was vulnerable and needed help
Though I pretended not to be
You saw right through me
I shunned you
I could be self-reliant
In a minute, I would be strong again
Even stronger
"Put your hand down," I said
"Go away!"
I searched my inner being for all that I needed to get up
And started to weep when it wasn't enough
I looked up and you stood there with your hand still extended
I reached out to you
You took my hand in yours
You braced me and carried me
Under your support, I started to rise
And not just rise
Climb heights unattainable before under my own strength
And then I knew
I needed you
You were my helpmate

Vacuity

I tried to fill my void
With money
With lovers
With philosophy
With causes
With religion
With mysticism
With success

And ended up emptier than before
But then I entered the sanctuary and I felt something
Something tangible
Living, breathing but not of flesh and blood
I felt spirit

But more than spirit – God
I felt the touch of the Almighty
He poured into me his totality
He took away the lacking, the missing, the almost
He gave me fulfillment in my empty places
He bridged my gaps
He rendered me wholeness

Joie de vivre - El Simchat Gili

Sometimes I have to dance
And sometimes I have to shout
Sometimes I have to wave my hands
Sometimes I just cry out

You leave me so euphoric
In splendid rapturous bliss
That I could run away with you
Not caring if I'm missed

You have me flying without wings
My spirit it does soar
I relish in our closeness
Our affaire d' amour

I find you so delightful
For you my passion burns
You set me all a flame my dear
From you I'll never turn

What heighten heights you've brought me!
What mountaintops and peeks
With you I feel such beauty
Exquisite and unique

With you I do hear joy bells
My eyes do have a spark
You gave me my salvation
You pulled me from the dark

I'll reach for you forever
You are my turtledove
My feelings they engulf me
I overflow with love

One day the trumpet will blow
I'll meet you in the sky
Rejoice with you eternal
The apple of my eye

Intimacy

In the stillness
In the calm
When all is tranquil
And there's silence
I feel your presence
And start to worship

And through the worship
You know I love you
I can feel your spirit
It enlarges my heart
It sets my being aglow

And it is a good thing
Wholesome, real, and authentic
And it is good thing
Holy, marvelous, and kind

And I feel so cherished
Like a child kissed on the cheek at bedtime
This is true intimacy

It humbles me
That you would even call me by my name
Would call me to worship
And for that I am so grateful
And for that Lord I will always enter in

Who You Are

You're not church or religion
Incense, chimes, or bells
You're not dogma, nor tradition
Utopia or hell

You're more than all the holy books
The alters and the shrines
You're more than prayer and miracles
Great wonders and great signs

The width, the breath, the depth of you
Too much to be revealed
You're more than intellect can bear
Or something that we feel

You're more than what we fathom
Accept or push aside
You're more than all we understand
And what we recognize
You're God

Loose

Heal me on the Sabbath day
Too long I've been so bound
Contorted by this spirit
Bent over to the ground

Tell me is the sky still blue
The clouds as white as snow
And do the stars still shine at night
Of this I'd like to know

I thought that I could handle it
At first the weight seemed light
Then crushing was the full impact
Stronger than my might

My soul is so disfigured
So twisted and contused
But if I can just touch you
I know that I'll be loosed

Heal me on the Sabbath day
Too long I've been so bound
Contorted by infirmities
Bent over to the ground

Storms

Light flashes through the darkness
The winds wail and blow with force
Raindrops race with vigor to touch the ground
While the sound of rolling thunder rumbles in the air
I see you in the storm
Your mercy and your power
Your compassion and your judgment
Your peace and your vengeance
Your gentleness and might
Is it any wonder?
That though I seek shelter
Truly I want to run outside while it's pouring
Getting soaked and wet
Embracing the storm and all that it brings with it
Becoming drenched
Having the waters drip down my face
And down my fingertips as I lift my hands in praise
Others long for balmy days
But I welcome the rain
Let the winds whirl and the thunder roar
The rain reminds me of you
So let it pour

Sing

Seraphim, Seraphim
And heavenly beings
Know what you better do
You better sing

Sing about his holiness
His mercy, his grace
How his glory is so brilliant
That you cover your face

Lift voices in unison
Be sweet to his ears
Til the loveliness is unbearable
And causes tears

Sing about his matchlessness
In all the earth
How you searched all the galaxies
And not found his worth

Sing him a love song
Til the worshipers cry
With a sound that's so reverent
That it shakes the sky

Seraphim, Seraphim
And heavenly beings
Know what you better do
You better sing

Like Gideon

Why do I keep stalling, stalling
Whenever I hear you calling, calling
For me to be what I'm supposed to be

Why am I not like the others, others
My sisters and my brothers, brothers
Who walk so boldly into their destinies

My confidence keeps abating, abating
And yet you keep waiting, waiting
For me to muster courage to take one step

You're relentless in your believing, believing
That one day I'll be achieving, achieving
Defying the monsters
That say I am inept

And though I cry God, God
What you ask is so hard, hard
I really can't believe what I've confessed

Cause when I seek your face, face
And put trust in your grace, grace
My struggle ceases and I'm given rest

So Lord let it begin, begin
Forgive me of my sins, my sins
Of stubbornness and bountiful doubt

I'll pick up this horn, horn
And like Gideon blow on, on
Trusting providence to naturally work
things out

If I would just yield, yield
And be a fertile field, field
My harvest would be plenty this I know

So break up my harden ground, ground
I'll plant my seeds deep down, down
So I can reap
My future you have sowed

This Love

This love explains everything
But remains an enigma
It's like healing to the fatally wounded
It's the longest embrace
It's a serenade
This love can be so ardent it's frightening
You want to flee it, but have to stay
Sometimes it feels like bondage, but it is total liberation
It purges and cleanses
It leaves you refreshed
It restores the shattered
This love gets in the soul and illuminates it
This love doesn't shame you when you are naked
Nor takes advantage of you when you are vulnerable
This love calms the restless spirit
This love makes you feel like a newborn nursing at mother's breast
And when you fail like we all do sometimes
This love encourages, forgives you and lets you try again
It gives you time to repent and find your way
This love resuscitates
This is God's love

You Know Me

What I tell the world
What I keep inside
When I've told the truth
And when I've lied

What lines I'll cross
What keeps me still
What empties my soul
How I am fulfilled

What I don't believe
What I dare to dream
What keeps me silent
What makes me scream

The roads I've traveled
Where I haven't been
Days of virtue
And nights of sin

All the things that I want to be
What others miss
And cannot see
You know me

Rocks

Cry out anyway
Because he's worthy
Cry out anyway
And give him praises
Cry out any way
Hosanna, Hosanna
Cry out any way
To the Rock of Ages

Cry out anyway
To the maker of all things
Cry out anyway
To the redeemer of men
Cry out anyway
To Leviathan's tamer
Cry out anyway
To the forgiver of sin

Cry out anyway
Like the angles above us
Cry out anyway
Like angels on high
Cry out anyway don't you dare be silent
Cry out anyway,
You betta cry

I Know Mary

And Mary said, My soul doth magnify the Lord,
And my spirit hath rejoiced in God my Saviour
For he hath regarded the low estate of his handmaiden: for, behold,
from henceforth all generations shall call me blessed.
For he that is mighty hath done to me great things; and holy is his
name. Luke 1:46-49

I know Mary
My soul like yours does magnify the Lord
And my spirit rejoices in God my Savior
He has shown this handmaiden the things of royalty
His scepter is always before me
He has given me the desires of my heart
He has caused me to sing a new song
My soul celebrates our relationship
He has rebirth me
I breathe him in like fresh air in the morning
Of all the things he will grant me
I desire most of him to forever bask in his glory
Let his glory shine on me like the warmth from the sun
How glorious is his presence!
Rebuking the rhetoric, heresy, and apostasy
I ask for feet that will always run swiftly to my first love
Let me not be like Othello taken in by lies
When Desdemona was oh so true
I know Mary, like you, he hath regarded the low estate of this
handmaiden
And hath done for me great things
Our souls do magnify the Lord

The Greatest

My soul is bare before you
With vulnerability
No bravado, no pretense
No barriers or walls
I let you see what I hide from others
I let you see where I haven't
Grown up
My immaturity
I let you see the range of my emotions
Disappointment and frustration
Anger and confusion
You can handle my darkness
My confessions belong only to you
When I was dead and stinking
You told me to come forth
From the cave that was my tomb
When I squandered my inheritance
In a foreign land
You didn't disown me
But gave me your fattest calf
And celebrated my return
You humbled me with your kindness
It was more than I deserved
You let me see when I was blind
And made me strong in my weakest moment
Falling in love with you was easy
And for me there is no greater love

Preacher

Preach on preacher, preach on
Preach bold and preach strong
Even if they leave pews
And get gone
Preach on preacher, preach on

Walk this preacher, walk this
Even if a few steps are missed
And there's pain mixed with the bliss
Press on, keep on, and persist

Cry preacher, go on cry
He ain't gonna answer all the whys
But he will wipe weeping eyes
So cry if you must, go on cry

Sure nuf preacher, sure nuf
You'll have to deal with a whole lot of stuff
Cuz life will try you, call your bluff
God or not you'll still get cuffed

But stand up, preacher, stand up
Even if the depths of hell erupt
And life's goodness leaves you abrupt
Lift your goblet drink from the cup

So preach on, preacher, preach on
Till your hairs are gray, robe worn
Till God takes you to the new morn
Yea, preach on, preacher, preach on

Infallible Proof

When I bend my knees and say a prayer
I know you hear me
When I don't know what to do
You counsel
When I've cried in sorrow
You've soothed me
When my mind is racing
You've given it serenity
When I doubt
You've given blessed assurance
Day by day you are there for me
I can feel your comfort
Like the heat from a fire burning on a cold winter night
I have no doubt
You are more than some idea swirling in my head
You are true
You are real to me

Dancing Before the Lord

David danced an open display of devotion
A not caring about appearances or interpretations
Just the need to be a worshipper
Breaking forth in the exaltation of you Lord
Enthralled in your Excellency
Surrendering self to your splendor
Engaging in the uninhibited act of praise
With full might he danced
Hungering only to please you
It was his way of expressing reverence
With clapping, and leaping and swaying
He danced just for you
Man with God
God with man
In communion
The way it ought to be
And David didn't care who couldn't understand
He didn't care who disapproved
He was dancing before the Lord
It was all for you
It was all that mattered

Tinsel

If I don't always fit the mold
If I don't do what I am told
And I don't behave when being scold
Am I still a Christian?

If I wear skirts above my knees
Dance all night at parties
And come home way after three
Am I still a Christian?

If I enjoy a glass of wine
Or hit your cheek when you hit mine
Or gawk when I see someone fine
Am I still a Christian?

Rhetorical questions do I ask you
The answer has been tried and true
God still loves me through and through
Yes, I'm still a Christian

Here's the biggest secret kept
If faith's only rules and steps
Then in vain poor Mary wept
There's much more to being Christian
Grasp the message of the story
Faith is not regulatory
Being perfect mandatory
We fall short as being Christians

Scratch the surface, take a look
All types of folks in that their book
Persons humbled not forsook
Grace is offered to the Christian

God searches all our inner parts
Looks at the layers of our hearts
Wipes the slates with brand new starts
It's the beauty of being Christian

Yes we deal in rights and wrongs
Get confused where we belong
East of Eden, Timshel song
We find our way at being Christian

Revival

One word
One touch
A whisper
Not much
Let me take in the breath
You breathe

Speak hope
Inspire
Encourage, lift higher
I want to
Bring in the sheaves

I need a revival
Come lift me up
Restore my soul
Refill my cup

Give my soul
Its jubilee
A taste of freedom
And liberty

Where the spirit of the Lord is
My soul revives
Dry bones do live
And come alive

Thankful

There was a woman with caramel skin
People said she talked too much
But I said she had a lot to say
I'm thankful for my momma's life

There was a man
Walking taller than his cane
That sustained him
He took the time to teach me wisdom
Though gone, I'm thankful for my father

There's a family
More interwoven
Then any piece of tapestry
They have learned to get over it quickly
And love deeply

I'm thankful for my family

There are friends
Their blood runs in my veins
The same as my siblings
I'm thankful for them

There are enemies
And adversarial situations
Making life hard
But ironically making me strong
So I remain thankful

But most of all there is you
Giving me rest
Living water and honey from the rock
When I sojourn in desert places
You are my oasis
For you God, I'm thankful

Adore

You are Adonai
I want to kiss your ring
You're worthy of the diadem
You're worthy to be king
Come sit between the Cherubim
Come rightly take your throne
Put on a robe of righteousness
One with precious stones
Oh give me a new mouth, my Lord
One with perfect praise
Wash me with hyssop
And teach me of your ways
Whatever it does take dear love
It's you I want to please
For when I was disheartened
My burdens you did ease
Oh take me to your kingdom
Where servants can be free
To fly just like the Seraphim
And give honor to thee

Endunamoo

Some say
That God is not omnipotent
That his power and his strength
Have limitations

But that I can't accept
See the life I have lived
Hasn't always been pretty
There have been some hard knocks

And I'm not talking about
One blow that knocks you to your knees
After you've been walking upright for years
And for the first time in your life you taste dirt

I'm talking about
Blow after blow
Until you are bludgeon in a fetal position
And still you get up again and again

Surely that type of resiliency is supernatural
Infused from an omnipotent God
Who nurtures the "never surrender" in you
Some may say, that's just the human spirit
I agree it is something done from the soul
Deep within
It is the essence of what is spiritual

With real brokenness, longsuffering

And anguish
You have to reach higher
To the divine in you
That's what gets you up
That's what keeps you standing

Your ashes could be blowing in the wind
But instead
You go to a beautiful strength
Something inside is so strong
It can only be called holy
Surely you know it is God

Youth

Gray strands streak my hair
And there are wrinkles on my hands
It's just life
And how life is
Yet, when I think of you
And how you have been so good to me
My eyes they twinkle
They are starry like young love
And my heart
Why it beats, like the pounding of a schoolgirl
A schoolgirl with a crush
You make my insides tremble
And I feel like springtime
Like yesterday when I was young

Dare I

Dare I love you so?
Enter into your loveliness
Relinquish my inhibitions
Wipe your feet with my hair

Dare I love you so?
That I'd speak of you boldly
Though stones may be thrown to silence me
I would gladly be harmed

Dare I love you so?
I'd lose everything for you
Be stripped of my identity
Just to gain your acknowledgement
Have you call me by a new name
Dare I love you so?

Oh, how do you love me?
Do I really want to know?
It wasn't those nails that kept you there
Yes, dare you love me so?

Knowing

The blowing of the wind
The way it touches skin
On hot summer daze
On the beach

The crying of the soul
When warmth pours into cold
And a spirit is free
From oppression

The laughter of a child
Who gives the biggest smile
Just playing

The opening of the eyes
When one does become wise
And revelation knowledge
Becomes vision

The human at the core
Who wants to be more
And walk the path to be better

The Holy Ghost's touch
That explains so much
But only to those
Open to receive

The way that I know you
The essence of what's true
And the incomparable beauty of worship

Blurred Vision

People say that you can't see God
But I don't know about that
Not seeing God is like not seeing love
Not seeing hope
Or determination
Not seeing the will to live
If you can see those things
If you can see goodness
If you can see inspiration
And aspiration
If you can see possibilities
You can see God

Messenger

God said this and God said that
Baby, Baby, you're just whacked
He's not smoking weed
He's not using crack
Or snapping the can on his third six pack

So what you said
Can't be from him
Cause you're talking crazy
Like flavored water Jim

Ain't revelation knowledge
Or an enlightening word
There's a difference between
Being spiritual
And being absurd

We're to be wise as serpents
And gentle as doves
Some things are just nonsense
And not from above

Now I've heard you
Now you can hear me
You said that God said it
But I disagree

Lost

Clap your hands three times and stomp
Turn in a circle once then jump
Light a red candle and lightly blow
Leap up high, stoop down low

Habitual
Rituals
Perfunctory praise
Without sincerity or passion ablaze
Feigned false jubilation nothing sincere
No emotions causing laughter, no emotions causing tears

Where is the love that lingered like jasmine sweet
Like rhythm in the music with a pulse and a beat
Where is the love that brought me to praise?
That filled my nostrils like cinnamon and sage

I could go through the motions
With traditional ease
But it leaves me restless and unappeased
Bring to my remembrance how awesome you are
My Immanuel
My Yoshua
Like the Shulamite woman, I search after thee
Have you seen my beloved?
Bring him back to me

There's a void and emptiness
That I can't stand

Come my beloved
Give me back my hand

What's going on?
This isn't real
I need more than ceremony
I need to feel

Give me permission
To step beyond the Vail
Let your presence restore me
Till I weep and wail
Till I cry renewed
No I won't pretend
I want what was lost
To be found again

I Want

I want to run among the moors with you like Heathcliff did with Cathy
I want to kiss your nail print and your wounded side
I want to give you priceless gems: rubies, sapphires, and tanzanite
I want to see your glory
I want to wash your feet then massage them in precious oils
I want to embrace your essence
I want to hear the heartbeat of your soul
I want to give you praises above those heard by angels
I want to truly worship you
I want to linger in your presence
I want to agape you
This is what I want

Requiem

Meet me at the end of time
The threshold of forever
Take me to eternity
Where angels fill the heavens

Sing to me a new song
With lyrics kind and tender
Sing to me a new song
Of dearth and tears no more

Show me New Jerusalem
Where war and strife can't enter
Take me to the place
Where evil can not dwell

Comfort all my love ones
Rock them in your bosom
Tell them it's alright
For I am almost home

Flying

I remember being fifteen
And writing in my diary
Dare I say God is not tangible?
Not doubting that you exist Lord
But not knowing if you knew that I did

And a few years later
Young and confused
Like a broken wing bird
That is no longer sure about flying
You came to me
Called me by my name
And attended to my injuries

You took care of me
You healed me
You took me to the heavens
Where the seraph flies
And said now spring forth
Spread those healed wings
And there I took flight
And there I believed

Praise

Being with you transcends flesh and blood
Tissues, sinew, bones, muscles, and ligaments
I have found this relationship to be more than intellect and reason
And far more than emotionalism
More than religion
More than anything that I know
It is love and yet more than love
It is a spiritual union with you my God
Soulful
It is human
It is being
It is human being
So much so that my insides praise you
Sometimes I can't stand under the glory of it
And the joy of knowing you drops me to my knees
And from there the depths of who I am I cry out "hallelujah"

Conquer

I'm unable to shed a tear
I'm unable to be angry
I'm almost numb inside
Still, there's this dull ache
That pulsates within

I know what this is
It's my warrior stand
My you won't break me
Declaration to enemies
Trouble and just times
Of pain

I won't smile
Cause then I'll be lying
But my head won't
Hang either

If you follow my eyes
You'll see them looking
Looking to the hills
Where my help cometh
My help cometh from the
Lord

If you look inside my eyes
You'll see anticipation
Not what you expected
No there's no sorrow

There's only hope See this too will pass

You wonder how I do this
Am I like Samson
With strength that can
Be cut away

Send your Delilah I don't care
Fact is I'll tell you my secret
You don't have to cajole me
It's in God's love

That's how I stand
When you betray me
With the sweetest of kisses
On my cheek like Judah

That's how I rise
Above the wounds of a friend
Or hell breaking out
Or trouble on every side
That's how I keep moving forward
Though the wind is contrary

See I've rested in God's bosom
And I've been under his wings
And when he holds me
Ah, when he holds me
I overcome
I conquer

Reborn

When I met you
And you took my hand
I stepped into a new beginning

It was like for the first time
My eyes were opened
And not only could I see
But I had vision

Air filled my lungs
With a freshness
That when I inhaled
I knew what it meant
To breathe

It was strange
I had the same face, same gestures
All the things of my identity
And yet, here I was
Like a newborn
Pushed out of the womb
With all the possibilities
Of new life

Glory

Sometimes I just close my eyes
And imagine heaven
I see your robe filling the temple
Your majesty is all consuming
Who can wear a diadem before you?
Is it any wonder that crowns are cast before your feet?
I don't care about pearly gates
Or streets of gold
All I want is to see your glory

I'm Yours

No one knows how deep this is
Not even me
I searched within myself to find an ending
And realized this is everlasting
My spirit is yours
I am yours
You have possessed me with your love
I know I'm free to go
But I won't
It would stop my heart from beating
I would go mad
You are my morning, evening and dead of night
I can't imagine a day without you
Take my hand and walk with me
Walk with me the length of my lifetime
And when my life is over
Walk me the length of immortality
I am yours

Taken

I've been taken by the wind
The air I breathe
Has taken my breathe away
Can anyone hear what I hear?
The wind song
It calls to me
I smile as the wind blows through my hair
Its caress is soft and light
With the warmth of the summer
It touches me
While I walk barefoot on hot sand

Songs of Deliverance

Your love makes me sing songs of deliverance
Songs that come up from my once captured soul
Songs about new beginnings
And new days dawning
Of jail cells being opened and emancipation
How I dance without shackles
How I clap with unbound hands
Yes, you have given me freedom
Your love is liberty
A place without bondage and oppression
Where I'm not entrapped or snared
By my mind
By what I'm supposed to be
Or by my weaknesses
By what people whisper, say, or think
Or the rituals of life
You've healed my issue of blood
Taken away my leprosy
And those that would have stone me
Have dropped their rocks and walked away
Your love makes me sing songs of deliverance
Oh, la, la, la
Oh, la, la, la
Songs of deliverance
Are the sweetness songs

Metamorphosis

When you are just living
In everyday life
And then you feel anointing oil
Being poured on your head
And it saturates your scalp, and runs down your face
What do you do?

When you didn't want anything else
But to walk and talk and be
But instead you're becoming, transforming
Evolving
What do you do with that?

Now that you can't point at religion
Or religious people
The priest, the rabbi, the reverend
Now that you can't point at the skeptic
The scientist, atheist, agnostic or theist

When the ideological and theological concepts all seem silly
When all that's left is authenticity
And you don't know what to do
Because preconceived notions no longer make sense
What then?

When it's just you and God
Nothing else and no one else
When you can't find your fig leaves
You're left with no coverings

No barriers
Shear defenselessness
Then what?

Then and only then
Take your white stone
And claim your name
Then and only then become

Keeper

My brother doesn't know what to do
Without tears he cries
He lives in half truths
He lives in half lies

God, God it's so hard
To take the hand
That's always drowning
in sinking sand

He's breathing stale air
His lungs have collapsed
Chest heaving while wheezing
He's smothered and trapped

His demons are contagious
I could claim them as my own
I could so easily be him
Confused and alone

It's too easy to slay him
With grave clothes bound
Prepare him for burial
Lay him down in the ground

When he goes to his places
Where the flames flare high
And returns burned and singed
And about to die

Be his kindred redeemer
The Shepard of lost sheep
Show him unconditional love
While he sobs and weeps

He's been put down too much
Belittled, disdained
There's been disparagement
Ridicule and shame

Take away his dark clouds
Warm him with the sun
Be the lifter of his head
Give him joy and laughter
For every tear he's shed

And when his days are ending
From a life that's been so tough
Hold him until he filled with love
And knows that it's enough

Ezekiel 34

I answer the phone
And what did I hear
A recorded preacher soliciting in my ear
He started with a scripture
Then he pushed his luck
Saying sow into his ministry
For two hundred bucks

So I hung up the phone
Sat back and took pause
Sorry wrong number
Call Santa Claus
Pure solicitation
Swindle and bait
It's that type of religious nonsense
That I really hate

God hold me back
These folks aren't ashamed
To bamboozle, manipulate and exploit your name
They pimp you out Lord
Like you walk the streets
Like judgment isn't coming
And you they won't meet

Ezekiel is calling, and he's calling aloud
But they can't hear a thing
With their heads in the clouds

We see them on television
And running government too
They feign the faith
But they're just using you
For power, and influence and money galore
Ezekiel is calling, Ezekiel 34

Demigod

What you doing with that robe?
What you doing with that crown?
What you doing with that throne?
Telling people to bow down?

Crazy, crazy, you're so crazy
You're crazy like a fox
You look down on everyone
And put them in a box

Dominance and prominence
Are both your daily bread
And terror chills my inside
From the thoughts that fill
your head

The adulation, admiration
Oh how you eat it up
From all your little "yes" people
Faking like you're not corrupt

Their silence is so golden
Cause with you they've made a deal
To wallow in inducements
So you they won't reveal

I will not be your worshipper
Only to God, I'll bend the knee
To give you reverence just one time

Would be the death of me

Yes I know that you have power
But you are not supreme
Herald, Herald, foolish one
All's not what it seems

God's splendor fills the temple
His holiness the air
His glory is his alone
Of it he will not share

God's virtue makes me worship
He's worthy of the praise
I see the beauty of his love
To him my arms do raise

But you, you're just a despot
A tyrant with no spine
Not worthy of exalting
Cause you are not divine

For God I won't just bow down
For him I'll lay prostrate
To him only give I honor
No matter what my fate

Vision

Sighing in resentment
Fighting discontentment
Because my dreams are deterred
Need a seer

Pity party meltdown
Spinning head goes round, round
Cloudy thoughts
Nothing does seem clear

Got to get to Selah
Got to get to my Jah
To take away the over cased skies

Make it plain what blinds me
Give me vision
Prophesy
I need a word
Given from on high

Fortunes

I get it you got it
You have diamonds and pearls
You're at the top of the pyramid
You own the world

I get it you got it
The golden touch
Your name is Ching, Ching
You own so much

I get it you got it
It's the move in your swag
Your life says it all
You don't have to brag

Yet there's something wrong
Deep down in your heart
There's a hole, there's a murmur
There's a wee little spot

I get it you did it
You traded your soul
You're just an apparition
You're playing a role

I get it, you don't want it
It's not what its worth

You can't feel the ground
You can't touch the earth
Not money, not fame
Not sapphires or gold
Not fans or groupies
Or all you've been sold

Mercy that's tender
Sheer peace of mind
People that love you
It's what you must find

Walking like Enoch
Standing like Paul
Living your destiny
Answering the call

You get it, you got it
It's the lilies in the field
It's the vulnerability
The salve that will heal

You get it, you got it
It's the helping a friend
It's the Sunday sermon
When the church says Amen

You get it, you got it
It's what money can't buy
But it will cost you something
Of that I can't lie

You get it, you got it
It is life's most hidden treasure
And the riches once found
Well you can't even measure

Ambrosia

Uganda, Uganda
Oh what a lost
Can you even fathom
How much the real cost

How vulnerable, how gentle
How trusting, how pure
Your lambs for slaughter
You easily lured

The sweetness, the kindness
The lovely, the joy
The laughter, the essence
All this destroyed

You served the liar
And sacrificed truth
Up on the alter
You've laid your youth

And for your actions
You expect wealth
Trusting the liar
You've cursed yourself

If you kill the harvest
If you kill the seed
The ground will be barren
With nothing but weeds

The dearth, the poverty
The lack and despair
Rachael crying for her children
But they are not there

Uganda, Uganda
Oh what a lost
Can you even fathom
How much the real cost

Not Complicated

It's just too powerful in its simplicity
It's just too beautiful in its simplicity
All the debate and the minutia
Just fades into irrelevancy
When God takes your hand
Palm touching palm
Fingers entwined
And you just walk with him
It's just that simple
Nothing more

Cape Diem

God I wonder
Do we really see the day we are given?
All the treasures 24 hours can bring
To be fully human in everything
The chance to challenge giants
And know somehow though they are bigger
And yes, they are stronger, still in a fight we can win

The chance to close our eyes and image angels
A chance to find beauty in life's holiness
The chance to find our own loveliness
The chance to search the inner souls of others

We can rise above, the beatings, the knock downs
The put downs, the mockery and embarrassment
We can still stand though we've fallen
And we can stay strong though weakened

We can say I love you to someone who needs to hear the words.
Acknowledge the forgotten
Encourage, inspire, and motivate

Find out what makes our hearts sing
We can sit at the feet of an orator
And hear words of wisdom
Laugh until we cry
Sing off key
Dance

We can plant our flowers
Move on after standing still too long
Cry on a shoulder if need be

Breathe in and breathe out

We can be loved
Make Love
Find love
Accept Love
Give Love

We can find our sacred places
Worship, meditate and just be who we are
With the day we can give ourselves some freedom
We can commune with you

Your Love Is Like

Your love is like the quiet of the morning
Your love is like Selah
Your love is like no explanation necessary
Your love is like refuge
Your love is like counting stars
Or looking at a full moon
Your love is like blatant honesty
Your love is like beauty in an ugly place
Your love is like scratching deeper than the surface
Your love is like forgiveness
Your love is like crying until you feel the healing
Your love is like being taken care of
Your love is like being lucid
Your love is like no more pretending
Your love is like a touch, a kiss, an embrace from the heart
Your love is like acceptance
Your love is like love

Wrestle

Rat, tat, tat
I'm about to lose that
That precious thing called hope
I'm slipping in this quagmire
For salvation I do grope

Hear me
Hear me now I say
To you my arms are stretched
Can you help me in my despair?
When I'm beat down and a wretch

Rat, tat, tat
Here's where I'm at
I hang like a preposition
At the end of a sentence - wrong
Am I your imposition?

When I've entered Adullam
When I'm hiding in a cave
With enemies in hot pursuit
And I desire my own grave

When life dreams and inspirations
Seem ridiculous and far
When I wonder who I am
When I wonder where you are

Will you be a fire for me?

For my cinders need a flame
All the soot and all the ashes
Want to blaze let loose untamed

Rat, tat, tat
I must believe that
Though the light keeps getting dimmer
Must hold on until it's bright again
Know that you can make it shimmer

I don't need a bed of roses
Or some mountain high to climb
I just need to wrestle angels
Till I'm given what is mine

Rat, tat, tat
I'm about to lose that
Dark cloud and so much doubt
Want to see a sliver lining
And when the sun finally comes out

So I'm climbing Jacobs's ladder
Climbing right to Jubilee
And I won't stop till there's freedom
Till the angels set me free
Rat, tat, tat

Creation

Could I fill the void with science?
If I never felt your touch
Cling to protons, neutrons
The cosmos
Subatomic particles and such

Many scribes
Many orators
And the wise ones of our times
Repudiate and denounce you
They don't seek
Say there's no find

Yet I shiver with the thought that I
Could live life with you unknown
Never experiencing your glory
You're my God, my very own

For them I have no answers
And I probably never will
I'm just glad I felt your presence
And its something I still feel

So no matter what is said
Beyond religion, science, and thoughts
Formulas and computations
And anything that's ever taught

I am of my Creator

Call me ignorant, obtuse
Throw your hands up
Shake your head
Go on say, my screws are loose

Doesn't matter
How I was created
The ways and means I do not know
I just know of a Creator
And of how he loves me so

Beloved

I am my beloved
And my beloved is mine
I drink you like nectar
You're the finest wine

Without your presence
I don't want to live
You are my surrender
So I freely give

All to you
The one I adore
You are my essence
I live you at my core

The road less traveled
Never thought like this
Ups, downs
Mixed pains and bliss

Through every hardship
You are always there
With tenderness that bathes me
I'm washed in your care

And when I was angry with you
And I turned my back
You wooed me till I loved again
Despite my attacks

So my beloved,
Keeper of my heart
No one can put asunder
Or tear us apart

I am my beloved
And my beloved is mine
I drink you like nectar
You're the finest wine

Your Love II

Your love is like coming out of the dark
Your love is like coming up from the waters
Your love is like not looking back
Your love is like only moving forward
Your love is like beauty found
Your love is like bruises fading
Your love is like necessary change
You love is like dancing wildflowers
Your love is like no more confusion
Your love is like stopping the nonsense
Your love is like getting serious
Your love is like waking up

God

Their God is religion
Their God is their creed
For tenets and dogma
They serve and heed

His God is a bottle
His God is a beer
His God is the liquor store
That takes all his years

Their God is their intellect
Their God is their minds
Ideological concepts
They worship divine

Her God is her yesterday
Her God is her past
Her God is the fading beauty
She tries to make last

His God is his power
His God is his fist
Supremacy and dominance
That's what gives him bliss

Their God is the spotlight
Their God is the fame
Their God is us knowing
To call out their names

Conservative, Liberal
Or right in between
Their God is their label
The way they are seen

Her God is her ambition
The top is her goal
Whatever the cost
Including her soul

His God is no God
Evolution and mutation
Genes, species
Big bang
And adaptation

Their God is their politics
Red right, left blue
Elephants and jackasses
That's what they hold true

His God is his money
His this and his that
He likes to show off
His wallet is fat

My God is my God
That simple, that complex
He's the God of my content
And the God of my context

Beyond

You love me beyond the nightfall
Beyond my place of no return
Beyond my self-destruction
Proclivities I yearn

You love me beyond the nonsense
That keeps swirling in my head
The trips I take to rabbit holes
The troubles that I wed

You loved me as Herald
You loved me as Saul
Jezebel and Pharaoh
With no light in me at all

You loved me through my cynicism
When I was reckless and vile
You loved me when my heart was ice
And had to thaw a while

What can I say to a love like that?
What can I say to that cross?
Only that I am thankful
You truly love whoever is lost

Caterpillars and Butterflies

You never taught us acquiesce
You never taught us fear
To bow our heads
Or look away
So how did we get here?

You never taught us to get by
Or make our due with less
You never said to step aside
While others get the best

You never planted seeds of doubt
And yet oh how they've bloomed
We're acrophobic
Insular
Why can't we leave our rooms?

You never told us to shut up
One utterance or word
And yet we stay so deadly silent
Unnoticed and unheard

Enchanted is the forest
The place we choose to dwell
Why can't we live all that we dream?
We're under some deep spell

If we could only trust the truth
And lay our burdens down

And scream a scream from deep within
Yes finally make a sound

We'd realize that our cocoons
Where not a place to stay
But twist and turn and then break out
To finally fly away

Pneuma

It's only in your safety
Do I rest and quiver weak
Lay down my burdens, drop my walls
Find my voice to speak

I trust you like no other
You have never sought my pain
Your foot is not upon my neck
And you are not my bane

The Lord takes me to a breathing space
Where I can get some air
Clear my head of noises
And yes let down my hair

The Lord takes me to a breathing space
Where I can feel the breeze
Hear the wind song's lyrics
Leaving me at ease

Lovely, lovely, oh so lovely
I do breathe you in
You are my resuscitation
You are my oxygen

Skin

I used to pick at scabs of skin
Watching as I bled
Those crimson sores
With drops of blood
Upon my flesh so red

I didn't understand that scars
Were signs my sores had healed
That scarring gave me closure
Like a door shut tight and sealed

I couldn't get pass all the trauma
The way my mind was blown
To move beyond my yesterday
The life that I had known

But when I came to you
For help
Your words did make me calm
And then you tended to my cuts
And put upon them balm

You gave me shelter
And peace of mind
A place that I could rest
And even in my wounded state
I knew that I was blessed

Us

You and I
Like green earth, blue skies
Day breaks, sun rise
And mornings

Just you, just me
Like the ocean breeze
The nights that tease
The dawning

Right here, right now
You leave me so wowed
Where else can I find this?

So deep, I feel
My heart stand still
Such warmth and tenderness

To praise on high
Prostrate I lie
I reverence who you are

For sure, I'm clear
Lucid, my dear
Evermore, evermore my star

To you I cling
Wanting nothing
But for you to take me higher

All days that pass
Greater than last
With devotion that won't tire
Worship, I will
Until, until
Everlasting is no more

Forever bind
Our souls, our minds
And let our spirits soar

Hell

Torture, Anguish
Screams that won't end
Beauty removed
Justice for sin

Comeuppance
Vengeance
Removal of grace
Flames never ceasing
Is there such a place?

Moaning and groaning
Mercy that's lost
No chance for redemption
Oh what a cost

Demons and devils
Where the soulless dwell
Fire and brimstone
They call this hell

But I think it's much deeper
Like having no air
To feel without feelings
Love without care

To lose God forever
This is true pain
To not feel his glory
That's hell and its flames

I hope for heaven
Where God is the light
Where I can behold him
Stand under his might

With our finite knowledge
Of life and universe
We have no idea
Of hell's real true curse

The burning, the yearning,
The cries and the weeping,
The nightmares that won't stop
The lurking, the creeping

The emptiness, the void
The lonely hours
Discontentment and depression
The strength of dark powers

The chaos, the mayhem
All unbearable too much
The lost of love
The absence of touch

People fear the fire
They fear the flames
I fear you not coming
When I call your name

There is no other hell
At least not for me
Than the separation from God … For eternity.

The Knowing

I'm not a believer
It transcends that
I know that God is
It's not abstract
It's concrete

I've never seen a burning bush
Nor a withered hand restored
But I have had my midnights turned into mornings
And in the mist of confusion things have become clear
I've been exalted right in the middle of being beaten down
And have held on to joy through a heavy heart

Sometime humanity stops being human
Vanity replaces what is really beautiful
Stupidity is called genius
Vulgarity is called art

And what people have is more valuable than who they are
Those are the times that God calls me in
He shifts my perspective
He rescues my hope
He never lets cynicism possess me

The same way I know there is good in the world
I know there is a God in the world
I just know

Modern Day Pharisee

You're the master of the spin
Are you sure you're not in sin
Better do some re-pen-tin
Before you knock and won't get in

Here's a little revelation
Focus on your own salvation
Humility before elevation
You're the one needs transformation

Mirror check your looking glass
Don't you know we see your mask?
So much makeup what a task!
All that pretense it can't last

Always claiming to be Christian
But hell-bent on your own mission
You've made faith a coalition
Using God for recognition

From that soapbox step on down
Hush your mouth don't make a sound
Leave the sky, touch holy ground
Hypocrisy will keep you bound

Your Love III

Your love is like the quiet of the morning right before the day begins
Your love is like the still of the night
Your love is like hope when you've been so discouraged
Your love is like taking off sackcloth
Your love is like trusting in love again
Your love is like grief subsiding
Your love is like perfect timing
Your love is like leaving when you should
Your love is like crying with tears held back too long
Your live is like a sigh of relief

Christian

I am a Christian
I declare and say
It is not my religion
In any kind of way

It's a lifestyle
That I choose to live
Christ gave his life
So in turn I give

Him my devotion
And a love that real
Attraction that's so strong
Like magnets pull on steel

He orders my chaos
My inner wars do cease
Mayhem surrenders
And I'm given peace

You are all my exhale
You are what I breathe in
I am ever yours and I am a Christian

Spirituality

How many of us have gone beyond the Vail to commune with you
God in our humanness?
How many of us have sat with our souls?
Listened to the wisdom of the Holy Ghost
Let light pour into our dark places?

How many of us walk in humility and gratitude?
Use the power we have like sunshine to spread warmth on coldness
How many of us yield to meekness and would fight for justice?
How many of us transcend and let our old selves die?

How we help others and ourselves
How we inspire, how we encourage and give hope
To nurture, to protect, to care, to welcome
To yield to the inner most truths residing within
This is spirituality and this is true religion

Daystar

It's a night
With a darkness
So black
You are blind
And bad thoughts
Haunting, taunting
In the depths
Of your mind

Oh could have been(s)
And should have been(s)
Time has made all things past
But you can't live in your present
For your yesterdays still last

You are tormented
You are suffering
And you shrill at the night
You know there's a morning
Can you get to first light?

You reach out for tomorrow
But it seems so far
Long are the hours
Leading to the daystar

But you fight the twilight
Won't surrender to the dusk
You can reach your morning

You have to, you must

Redefine who you are
What you've been, what you can be
Touch the spirit of the Lord
Can you feel liberty
Daystar shine, daystar shine
When the night won't let go
Guide us till day does break
And all glory does show

Figs

God your people are always talking about breakthrough, breakthrough
When all I really want to do is breakout
Can I escape the rhetoric?
I'm sick of it
The blah, blah, blah
Can you take me far?

From all they claim
In your name
And just give me solace
The pontification
Is suffocation

Want to scream stop
From a mountain top
Where have the true prophets gone?
Did they choose dusk instead of the dawn?
What happened to thus said the Lord
Can we really afford?

To put on Mona Lisa faces
Never showing traces
Of broken hearts
Like puzzle parts
Needing to be put together
Whatever
Not making amends
We rather pretend

Holy, holy, holy
As our souls die slowly
We'd rather fake it
Instead of being naked
Our nudity is too much to bear
So our fig leaves we continue to wear

Needy

What can I say?
I need you
I won't pretend that it's not true

Like oceans need water
Like crops need rain
Like warmth needs heat
And the heart needs to beat

What can I say?
I need you
I won't pretend that it's not true

Like diamonds need coals
Like the earth needs the sun
Like words need a voice
Like decisions need a choice

What can I say?
I need you
I won't pretend that it's not true

Like mercy needs grace
Like wounds need to heal
Like thoughts need the mind
Like compassion needs kind

What can I say?
I need you
And I won't pretend that it's not true

Hand Holding

If you take my hand
I can walk on the wings of the wind with you
If you take my hand
I can discover what pure love feels like
If you take my hand
I can surrender
If you take my hand
I can let go of my fears
If you take my hand
I can be courageous
If you take my hand
I can let my walls crumble
If you take my hand
I can heal
If you take my hand
I can begin the beginning
If you take my hand
I can end the ending
If you take my hand
I can just live
If you take my hand
I can work through the sadness
If you take my hand
I can face the madness
Oh, if you take my hand

All That's Divine

It's the quiet in the morning
When the first bird sings
It's the blooming of the trees
That signal spring

It's the outburst of laughter
With joy and mirth
It's the pain and the pleasure
Of giving birth

It's the milestones of life
That you can't forget
It's the moving forward
With no regrets

It's not even conceivable
With the human minds
The beauty of holiness
And all that's divine

Beautiful Ugly

Lord I saw the beauty of the ugly
And it left me quite amazed
Hypnotic and alluring
I was spellbound in a haze

Can't get caught up in the power
Of the prominence so sweet
And taste of the forbidden
Just because its there to eat

There's no wonder
That the elders 24 did drop their crowns
And instead of exaltation
Chose to humbly bow on down

There are peaks that are real valleys
There is light with darkness deep
There are wolves but you can't you see them
They're pretending like they're sheep

Allured by what is charming
The temptation such a tease
Like a rodent with no thought
Of the mousetrap with its cheese

Humble me before the humbling
Bring me down before I fall
Let me see the truth before me
There's no beauty here at all

Take me out of this black darkness
Even if it hurts my eyes
Even if the light is blinding
No more spellbound, hypnotize

Want the beauty of the truth
Though so ugly it can be
Rather rest in what is real
And maintain authenticity

Kite

Holy Ghost come
Come mighty wind
So I may be carried high
It's only through your ushering
Am I am able to fly

Let me dance to your wind song
Blow wind, blow
Up to the heavens
Where the winged ones go

Let me soar
Higher, higher
Let nothing get me down
Let me rise above my strongholds
Let nothing keep me bound

Lift me up, lift me up
Blow your wind until I rise
High enough to touch glory
To be one with your skies

Emancipation

I hear them as they talk
They bicker and they squawk
Of liberty
And hands they want unshackled

Should I let them be?
Or tell them you're the key
That opens every lock
That keeps them bound

See prison can be sweet
A place the soul retreats
Where lies are soothing
When truth is just too harsh

See freedom has its price
But few will sacrifice
And live the life
That emancipates the living

Most of us can't handle
We're the flame that lights our candles
In our own darkness
We've forgotten how to shine

But in your brightness, make us brilliant
Liberated and resilient
Teach us how to keep our flames
For ever burning

Guide us on Pillar of Fire
To the place our heart aspired
No Egyptian, no enslavement
We are free

And when darkness brings enticement
Let us shun it with enlightenment
No longer are we captives
We're set free

Word

And the Word was God

When you speak to me
I can breathe again
My heart just overflows
When you speak to me
I am all that I am
And my lovely starts to show

When you speak to me
I am ethereal
And I float upon the air
When you speak to me
I am special
Like red diamonds oh so rare

What you speak to me
It's a lovely song
Your lyrics bring me healing
And gives me hope
In spite of wrongs

Broken

For real you want me to dance like this
My bones are broken and I'm in pain
For real you want me to dance like this
In the storm and in pouring rain

Where is the beauty you promised me?
My ashes weigh me down
Is this the test of steadfastness?
Before I get my crown

My eyes are weary from weeping
So blurred I cannot see
Is this the cross you mentioned?
If I would follow thee

My heart I freely gave to you
My spirit opened wide
And in my deepest darkest places
I let your light reside

Those dry rotted bones without marrow
Somehow you made them live
And though I couldn't give you much
I gave what I could give

So I'll dance in brokenness
Till all my bones rejoice
Till there's healing rains from heaven high
And you give me back a voice

Till the ashes turned to beauty
Till the storm surrendered peace
Till I inhaled joy like fresh air
And my sadness it does cease

Mother's Cry - The Hoodie Song

Rachael, Rachael God isn't sleep
He hears when you groan
For that beautiful boy
Senselessly stoned

The one that didn't make it
Down the river Nile
But like the wind
Stayed just for a while

Though they justify the hanging
When they hung him high
Rizpah stand strong
Make them hear your cry

Beautiful boys, beautiful boys
Not living the lives that they could
Slain for stupid stuff
Like wearing hoods

So Loved

God said
Here I am
There they are
Too much distance
Way too far
Want my hand
To them reach
Must find way
To close breach

Jesus said
Here I am
Send me down
Humble me
Take my crown
Let me die for their sins
Send them a Comforter
To dwell within

Bible says
At the cross where blood dripped
When Christ died the vail ripped
No more gap or separations
John 3:16 the proclamation

Heaven

They say the streets are paved with gold
But I don't care
They can be dirt roads
As long as you're there

They say there are mansions
Houses supreme
Opulence
Beyond our dreams

But heaven is more
It's jubilee
It's the ultimate grace
God's place of charity

To illuminate his spirit
To connect with his heart
To join in righteousness
To never part

To worship, to praise
To magnify
A place where his sovereignty
Is held on high

A place where the angels
And man can sing
Glory, glory
To our King

Raw

Tick, tick tock
Goes the clock
Time to get up
Life interrupt
With a real life
Cause what you been living
Ain't been life at all

Do what is deemed
Wake up that dream
With a loud noise
You've been too poised
Rock that boat
Before you choke
On your mediocrity

Do what is meant to be
You can handle the intensity
There's no shame
In moving in his name
And finally living and loving
Raw, real, and right

Speak to Me

Hush, I hear the calling, calling
Of the still small voice
That I once ignored
The voice I showed no reverence
And now I do adore
Holy, holy, holy
How the whisper sings
Oh how my heart does flutter
Just like angel wings
I humbly will follow you, the Great I Am
Into shadows and green pastures
Let me be your lamb
Speak quietly, speak softly
But let me hear
The voice of the Good Shepard
That I cherish so dear

Shine forth

I know that's how you saw me
But that's not who I am now
It's not my fault you never took a second look
And you're more comfortable if I still pretend
To be less than
So that you can be more than
Cause you can't handle
That I'm who God says I am

So no, I don't want to applaud you
Just because you want to take a bow
You never wanted me strong
Or beautiful, or respected
I am all those things and more
I am who God says I am
I can no longer feed your insecurities
I can no longer feed my own

I chose to live in shadows
I chose to hide my talents in the dirt
I walked with false humility
Since I wouldn't give God glory
You took his glory for yourself
And I let you

We both blaspheme
But I have to give God glory today
I have to let him shine forth
And that means

Shining forth through me
Being his vessel
We both can
Your light doesn't dim mine
My light doesn't dim yours
Let's both shine

Our Story

No greater love
The sweetness, oh how kind
Oh, the beauty, utterly divine
What a wonder, to know you exist
To feel your spirit
Oh, Lord how can I resist
The chance to worship
To fill my heart with your glory,
This time belongs to us
This is our story

Gravity

With you there is no gravity
I'm not scared to fall
With you I am flying high
Feeling like I have it all

With you nothing brings me down
Well at least not for long
Cause you lift me up
When tears do come
And help me to be strong

With you there is no gravity
So I rise not being afraid
Rising above my limitations
And all the mistakes I've made

You freed me from my birdcage
I'm in bondage no more
My naysayers look up and see me
Watch me fly, watch me soar

The sky is beneath me
The mountains peaks so low
And still you lift me higher
To heights I didn't know

Higher, higher, up to heaven
Firmaments I've never seen
Where your love is felt the greatest
And everything's serene

What if

What if it's about feeding the hungry?
What if it's about being kind?
What if it's about spreading the gospel?
What if it's about walking the line?

What if it's about loving your family?
What if it's about marriage vows kept?
What if it's about sharing love?
What if it's about showing some depth?

What if it's about sacrificing?
What if it's about getting things done?
What if it's about facing music?
What if it's about deciding not to run?

What if it's about playing it forward?
What if it's about lending helping hands?
What if it's about showing some empathy?
What if it's about trying to understand?

What if it's about letting God be God
What if it's about a servant's heart?
What if it's about beginning the beginning?
What if it's about just making a start?

Still

Without morality there is still God
Without creation there is still God
Without a personal relationship with him
Again, there is still God
Without the bible and scriptures there is God
Without reasoning and explanations there is still God
Without believers there is still God
Without prayer, without praise and without worship from me or others
God still exist

Reality

Some folks say loving you is silly
Like trying to love the wind
The fallacy of you existing
It's what they call a sin

Yet, I have touched the hand of God
In fact, I've held it tight
I have walked like Enoch striding
Transcended in the light

I have felt my own redemption
And the sigh of a soul released
And in your name slain inner demons
Put a dagger to some beast

You have strengthened me in my weakness
You've rebuilt my leaning wall
You have carried me at my lowest
And helped me when I've crawled

I can always feel the shining
Of the Holy Ghost inside
Benefactor of the ripped veil
Split and opened for me wide

So what can I say to Agrippa?
And those that shake their heads
Who feel the bible is fiction
A storybook that's read

I can only say I'm raptured
And my chariot has fire
That I'd throw my crown before him
And much more that I've acquired

There's a river running through me
Living water flowing free
And this life is the illusion
But my God reality

Awaken

How long have I been sleeping?
Heart and mind comatose
Lethargic inertness
Unconscious overdose

Caught up in nothingness
Absent sensory
Thought I was living - not
Trapped in a reverie

How can I awaken?
Escape from this dream
Want reality
Can't trust what is seen

Let me come out of this trance
Let me come out of this daze
Escape the labyrinth
Stop walking in this maze

Give me the red pill
I want to take it now
How far to the rabbit hole?
Not afraid to go down

Rather be awaken
Then in a dream world remain
Truth sets you free
Though there might be some pain

Taking up my bed at Bethesda
No excuse I am healed
Won't settle for the numbness
Now that I can feel

Eyes wide opened
Have had my time to rest
Rejuvenated, revived,
Restored, refreshed

Took a mighty long time
But now I have a clue
Revelation knowledge
I now know what to do

Gestation

Tick Tock
I looked on for so long
Wondering would I ever be
All the things you said I would be
Tick tock went the clock
I felt locked
Locked up in
Dreams castrated
Visions barren
And beliefs dried up
Yet, my maddening, tenacious and relentless faith
Wouldn't let me acquiesce
Nor take in the solace of surrender
Rest, yes
Take a drink by the brook, yes
But faith kept me yielded and bound
It knew and knows God's word cannot comeback void
So I press into due season
Knowing at the appointed time
Manifestation will give birth
To the promised of God

About the Author

Yvette Mulkey lives in a suburb outside of Washington, D.C., but still considers herself a Washingtonian. Whenever possible, she takes advantage of D.C. life whether dining in Georgetown or visiting one of D.C's. many museums.

She caught the writing bug when she was in the sixth grade. A story she had written was published in the school's newspaper. She knew then and there she wanted to be writer when she grew up.

While in college she read John Steinbeck's East of Eden and vowed she too would not shy away from difficult subjects such as social justice relationships and spiritualty. She enjoys poetry readings and though a self-proclaimed introvert she has participated in spoken word forums where she has read some of her poems. She has a background in marketing and communications and has worked as a content writer and editor of publications for more than 20 years.

www.ingramcontent.com/pod-product-compliance
Lightning Source LLC
Chambersburg PA
CBHW071456070526
44578CB00001B/354